Spelling Age 10–11

Rhona Whiteford

Rhona Whiteford has many years' experience of teaching at preschool and primary school level, and is the author of a wide range of educational books for teachers, parents and children. She has two children.

Consultant: **Andrew Burrell**

Andrew Burrell has worked as a primary school teacher and as a lecturer at the Institute of Education, University of London, and has carried out research into the teaching of Language and Literacy.

Illustrated by **Michael Evans**

About this book

This book contains spelling activities suitable for 10- and 11-year-olds. They are based on the National Curriculum and National Literacy Strategy requirements for Year 6.

The activities gradually become more demanding, so it is important to start at the beginning.

The spelling skills taught or practised in each unit are stated at the top of the page. A note at the foot of the page tells you more about the purpose of the activities and gives advice about how to help your child with them.

Stickers are provided as a reward and as a record, and the progress chart at the back of the book gives you a useful checklist of skills.

Each unit ends with a positive comment. Encouragement from you will work wonders, so be generous with your praise!

How to help your child

- Find a quiet place for your child to work, preferably sitting at a table. This will help concentration.
- Work with your child on a regular basis to maintain interest and motivation.
- Make sure your child has access to good-quality writing materials.
- Look at an illustrated children's dictionary and a thesaurus together. Looking at words helps with spelling skills.
- Play Scrabble and other word games and have fun with spelling quizzes.
- Encourage your child to check his or her work.

Above all, be relaxed – and have fun!

h

Hodder Children's Books

a division of
Hodder Headline Limited

Suffixes (1)

A **suffix** is a group of letters which can be placed at the end of a word to change its meaning.

1 Put each of these words into the correct bucket.

nation completion station motion contribution
repetition depletion devotion formation deletion
distribution translation revolution notion education
position excretion pollution lotion secretion
competition emotion opposition institution petition

... ation

... etion

... ition

... otion

... ution

The **relaxation position**!

Listing words with the same suffix (ending) will help your child to remember the spelling. Encourage him to look for the differences between the words as well as the similarities. Show him how to work methodically, crossing out each word as it is used up.

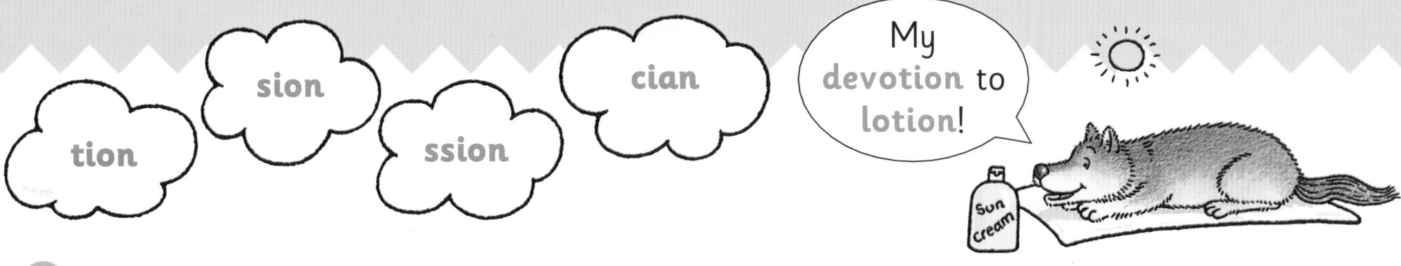

2 **Write a suitable caption under each picture.**

passion
mission

exclusion
confusion

lotion
motion

percussion
session

magician
optician

proportion
reduction

oppression
profesion

~~fraction
reduction~~

infusion
explosion

fraction reduction

Hi, Teach!

Discuss the captions before your child starts to write. The humour should engage his attention and help him to remember the spellings. Encourage him to scan the whole page, completing the easier questions first.

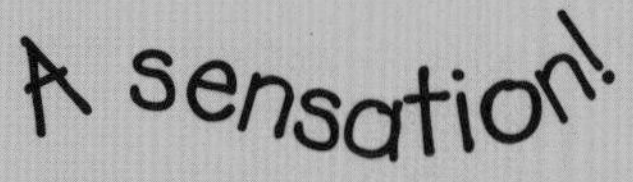

Root words

A **root word** is a word to which prefixes and suffixes can be added to change its meaning.

1 Look for the root of each of these words, and then list the words in "families" on the pots.

excellently triangle personal angled excelled uncover unfit
unclear justice fitted personally excellency covering personality
fittest personify rectangle injustice justification recover clearly
clearing refit adjust discover excelling quadrangle cleared

act		
	act	ion
	act	or
in	act	ion
re	act	ivate

angle		

just		

cover		

person		

excel		

clear		

fit		

Show your child how to scan the word bank, looking for words containing the same root. Look up the root words in a junior dictionary.

2 **Look at the root word on each of these two root vegetables. Using a dictionary, write ten words based on each root.**

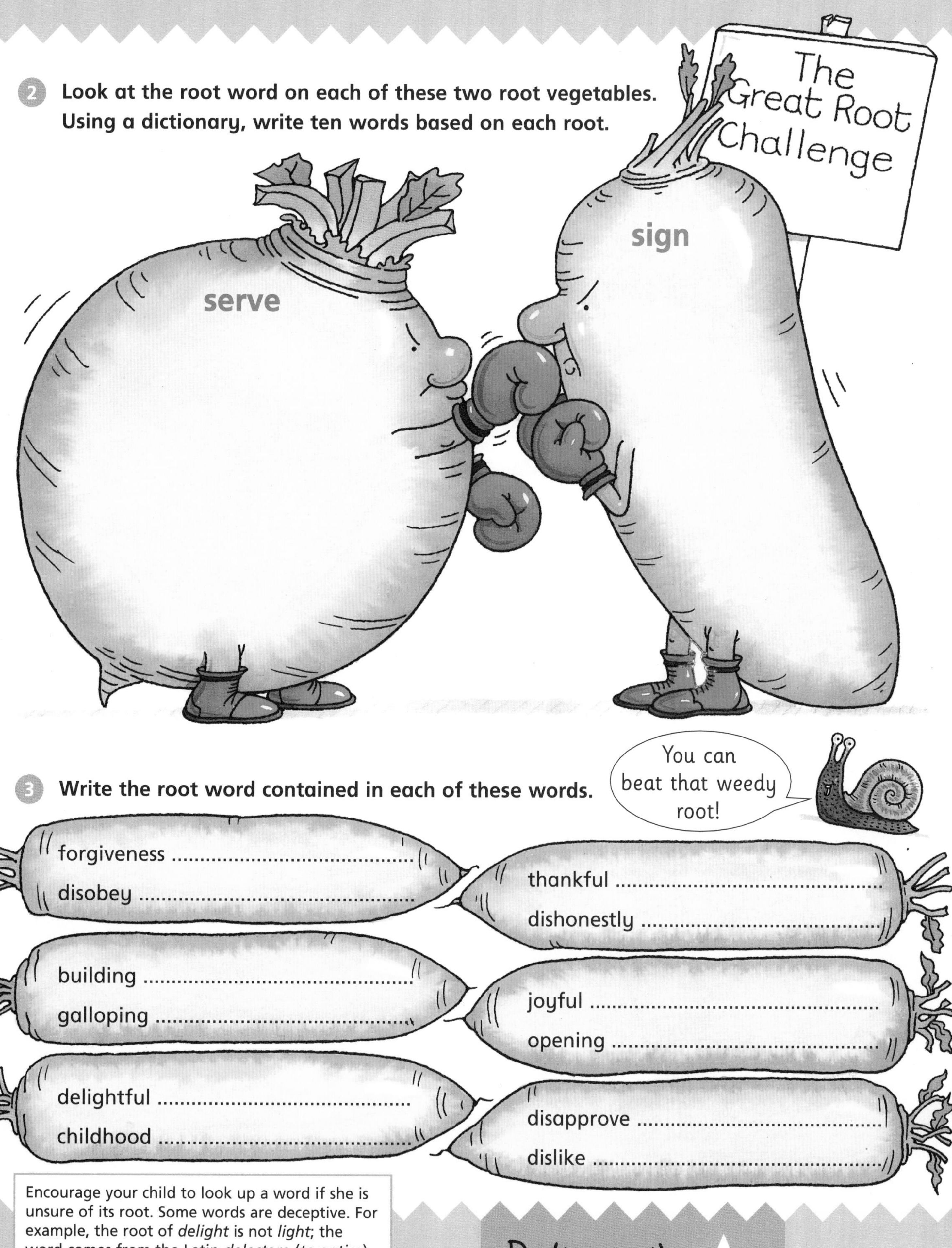

3 **Write the root word contained in each of these words.**

forgiveness ....

disobey ....

thankful ....

dishonestly ....

building ....

galloping ....

joyful ....

opening ....

delightful ....

childhood ....

disapprove ....

dislike ....

Encourage your child to look up a word if she is unsure of its root. Some words are deceptive. For example, the root of *delight* is not *light*; the word comes from the Latin *delectare* (*to entice*).

Suffixes (2)

1 Read this report and underline words which end in the suffix ial. Write the words in the box.

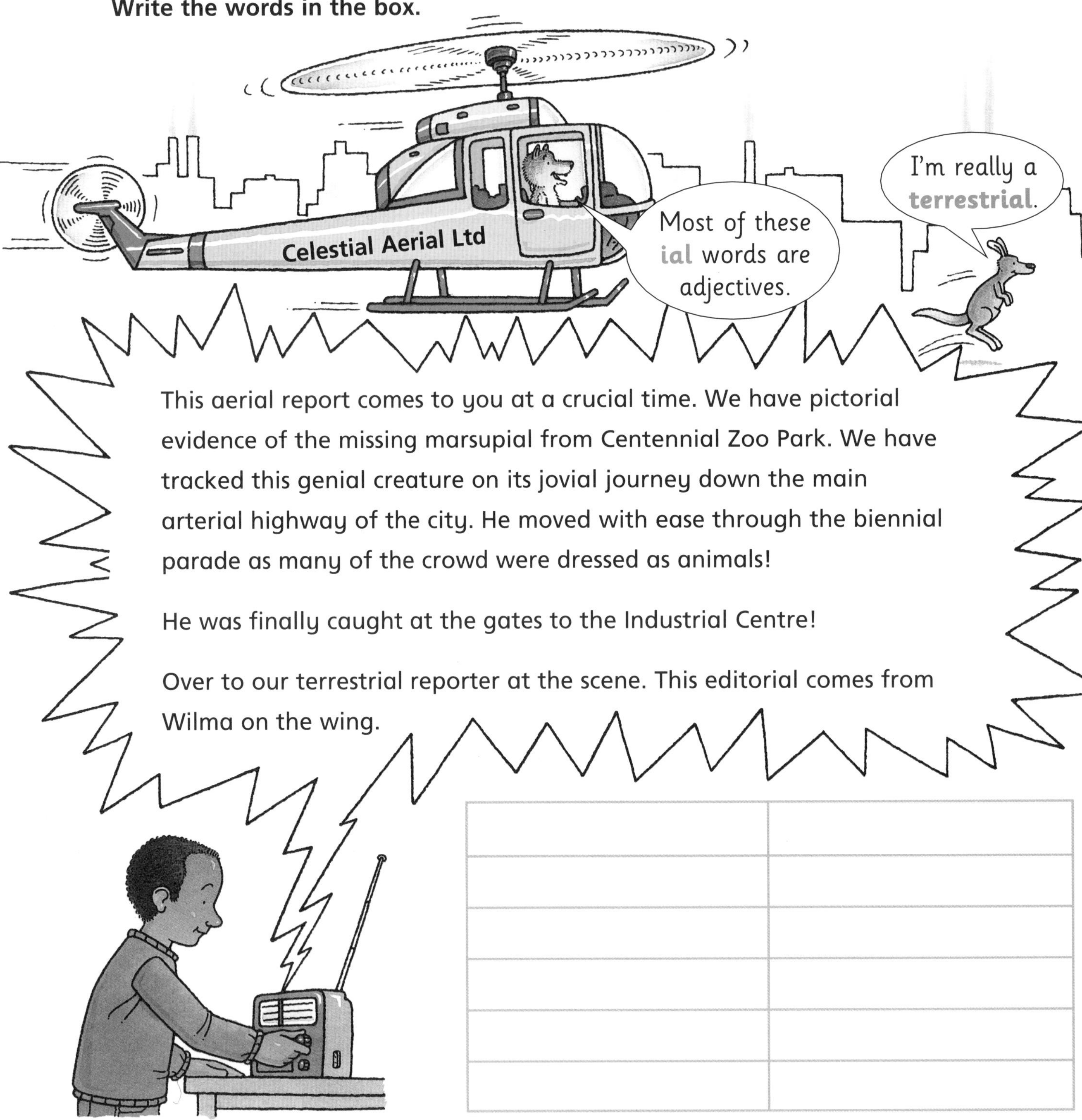

This aerial report comes to you at a crucial time. We have pictorial evidence of the missing marsupial from Centennial Zoo Park. We have tracked this genial creature on its jovial journey down the main arterial highway of the city. He moved with ease through the biennial parade as many of the crowd were dressed as animals!

He was finally caught at the gates to the Industrial Centre!

Over to our terrestrial reporter at the scene. This editorial comes from Wilma on the wing.

Encourage your child to keep a word log in a small notebook. He could list suffixed words, using a rhyming dictionary.
Take a page from a newspaper and have a race to underline words ending in *ial*.

2 **Make adjectives by completing each word on the ski slope with the suffix able. Then write the complete word.**

3 **Complete the speech bubbles with ible words from the cloud.**

visible sensible indestructible
possible irresistible collapsible
horrible terrible flexible

miser ....
....
prob ....
....
teach ....
....
avail ....
....
reli ....
....
enjoy ....
....
laugh ....
....
avoid ....
....
agree ....
....
wash ....
....

Are you **able** to ski from the summit to base camp?

V.........................!

P......................... but not s.........................!

He's ir.........................!

He's in.........................!

I'm f......................... and c.........................!

Try spotting invented words ending in *able* or *ible* (e.g. *doable, lunchable*) in advertisements. Encourage your child to make up some more (e.g. *snugglable*).

Incredible!

Prefixes

I can do **aerobatic aerodynamic aerobics**!

A **prefix** is a group of letters that can be placed at the beginning of a word to change its meaning.

aqua trans re pre

aero super mega pro

1 **Complete each prefixed word on the crosses below, and then write the word next to its definition in the table.**

port store wind sonic
historic plane lung noun

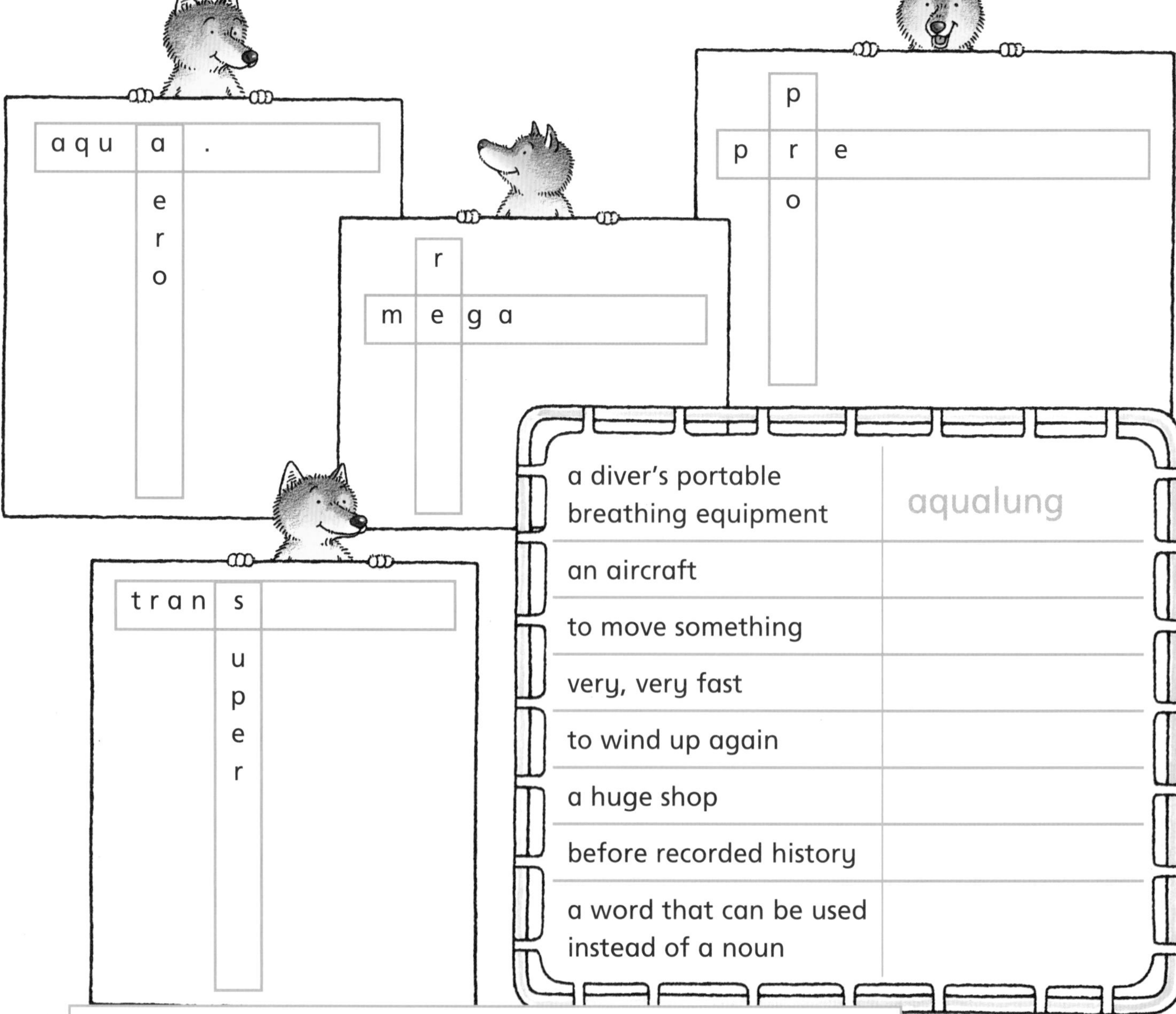

a diver's portable breathing equipment	aqualung
an aircraft	
to move something	
very, very fast	
to wind up again	
a huge shop	
before recorded history	
a word that can be used instead of a noun	

Encourage your child to check the meanings of prefixes and prefixed words in a dictionary. Some words appear to begin with a prefix but do not; for example, *premium* comes from the Latin word *praemium*, and the letters *pre* are not a prefix in this case.

2 Your computer has started to invent some prefixed words. Finish the job by connecting each prefix to a suitable root word. (The prefixes are printed in green and the root words in red.)

✓P.C.

re, aero, play, wet, bi, tele, aqua, photo, potty, angle, port, hat, octo, micro, music, run, surge, trans, gloves, film, duo, hydro, cycle, audio, auto, power, phone, super

A reconnection collection!

aquasurge!

duohat?

audiogloves

3 Use these prefixes and roots to make more unusual words. Write each word and illustrate four of the words.

✓P.C.

....

....

In Question 2, let your child use a different colour to connect each pair.

Using these prefixes, try to invent some futuristic 'gadgets' together. Here are some to start you off: *telefridge, autospoon, aeroshoes, audiopillow.*

Supertastic!

Suffixes (3)

Train your memory using one of these ideas.

1 Copy

Learn a group of words which have the same spelling pattern. Copy each word three times.

factory	*factory*		
conservatory			
laboratory			
exploratory			

Use a favourite script.

2

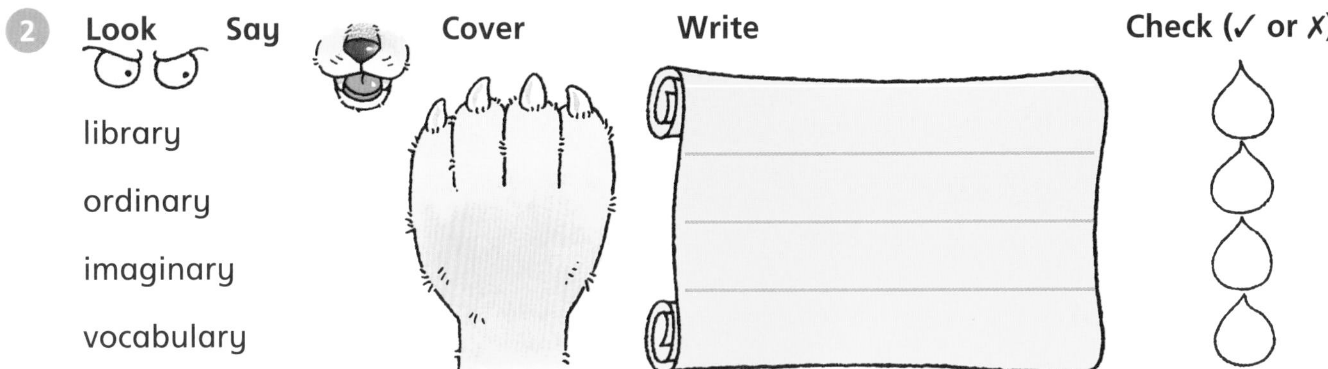

library

ordinary

imaginary

vocabulary

3 Patterns

Make the words into a pattern.

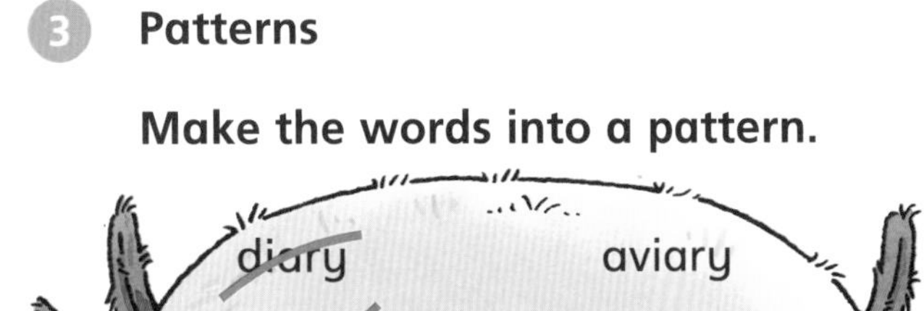

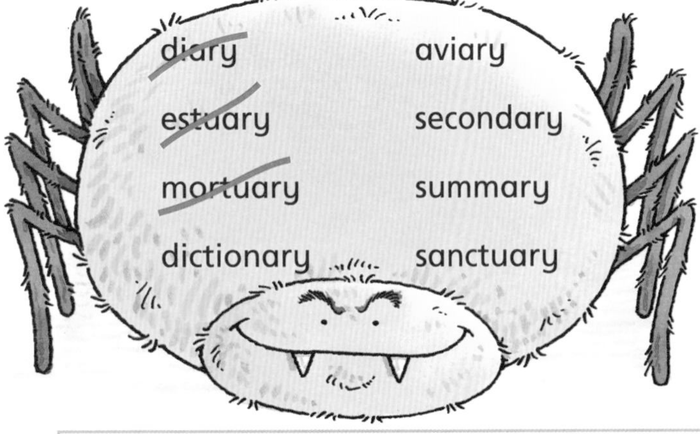

Another useful strategy for remembering spellings is to spell the word aloud. Try spelling out the beginning of a word and asking your child to complete it.

4 Syllables

Divide the word into syllables and then learn it. Cover it and then write it.

mach / in / er / y	
d i s / c o v / e r / y discovery	s t a t i o n e r y
c o o k e r y	f l o w e r y
p o w d e r y	p a p e r y
l o t t e r y	u p h o l s t e r y
s a d d l e r y	b u t t e r y

5 Word length

Write the words on squared paper and compare their lengths.

See how fast you can do it!

Wilma	W	i	l	m	a				
mercury									
century									
luxury									
treasury									
jury									
factory									
victory									
memory									
territory									

Using squared paper, make up a crossword together. Use only words which contain the same suffix. Make up the clues when you have enough words on your crossword grid.

6 Colours

Write the suffix of the word in blue and the root in red.

greenery rookery mockery
cookery trickery rockery
crockery witchery

Exemplary!

Join them up (1)

A connective is used to join two ideas.
It may be a single word … or a phrase.

finally   in other words

Some connectives are compound words.

however

1 **Underline compound words in blue, phrases in red and the other connectives in green.**

also   if   because   on the other hand   finally

furthermore   so   and   anyway   in addition to

for example   meanwhile   however   in other words   yet

2 **Split each of these compound words into separate simple words, then cover the word and rewrite it from memory.**

more/over	moreover	meanwhile	
whatever		furthermore	
whoever		whenever	
therefore		anyway	
however		besides	
whereas		nevertheless	

I'm taking the dog for a walk, although it looks as if he's taking me!

A connective can link parts of a sentence or two separate sentences. Not all connectives are conjunctions (e.g. *and, but*).

Encourage your child to try to spot connectives in everyday conversation and in newspapers.

3 **Underline the connectives and then write them below.**

Connectives

....

....

....

....

....

....

....

....

....

Let your child make a collection of connectives. She can then refer to them when she is writing. Connectives are particularly useful in constructing an argument.

Brilliant! ★

Suffixes (4)

Some suffixes can change:

an adjective to a verb		a noun to an adjective		a noun to a verb	
quiet	quieten	wood	wooden	advert	advertise

ify en ate ise

1. **Add en to each adjective to make a verb.**

black........... soft...........

tough........... hard...........

deaf........... dead...........

2. **Add en to each noun to make an adjective.**

silk...........

gold...........

lump...........

3. **Add ise to each noun to make a verb.**

glamour........... terror...........

capital........... symbol...........

You will need to change the endings of these nouns before you add ise.

pressure........... memory...........

sympathy........... summary...........

4. **Write each verb next to the noun it comes from.**

Nouns

vaccine .... liberty ....

narrator .... orchestra ....

celebrity .... gravity ....

decor .... medicine ....

Verbs

vaccinate narrate
celebrate decorate
liberate orchestrate
gravitate medicate

Your child should be able to cope with the fairly sophisticated verbs on this page. Try to use adult language in conversation, and always explain any difficult words he comes across. This will help to broaden his vocabulary.

5 **Underline each verb ending in ify in red, and the corresponding noun in blue.**

The notice was written to notify everyone of the discovery.

They had started to mummify the body but it was not yet a mummy.

She had great beauty and did not need make-up to beautify her.

The identity of the cat was unknown as there was no one to identify him.

This is a TV game which tests intellectual and physical skills.

6 **Read this notice. Underline verbs which end in ify, en, ate or ise in blood red!**

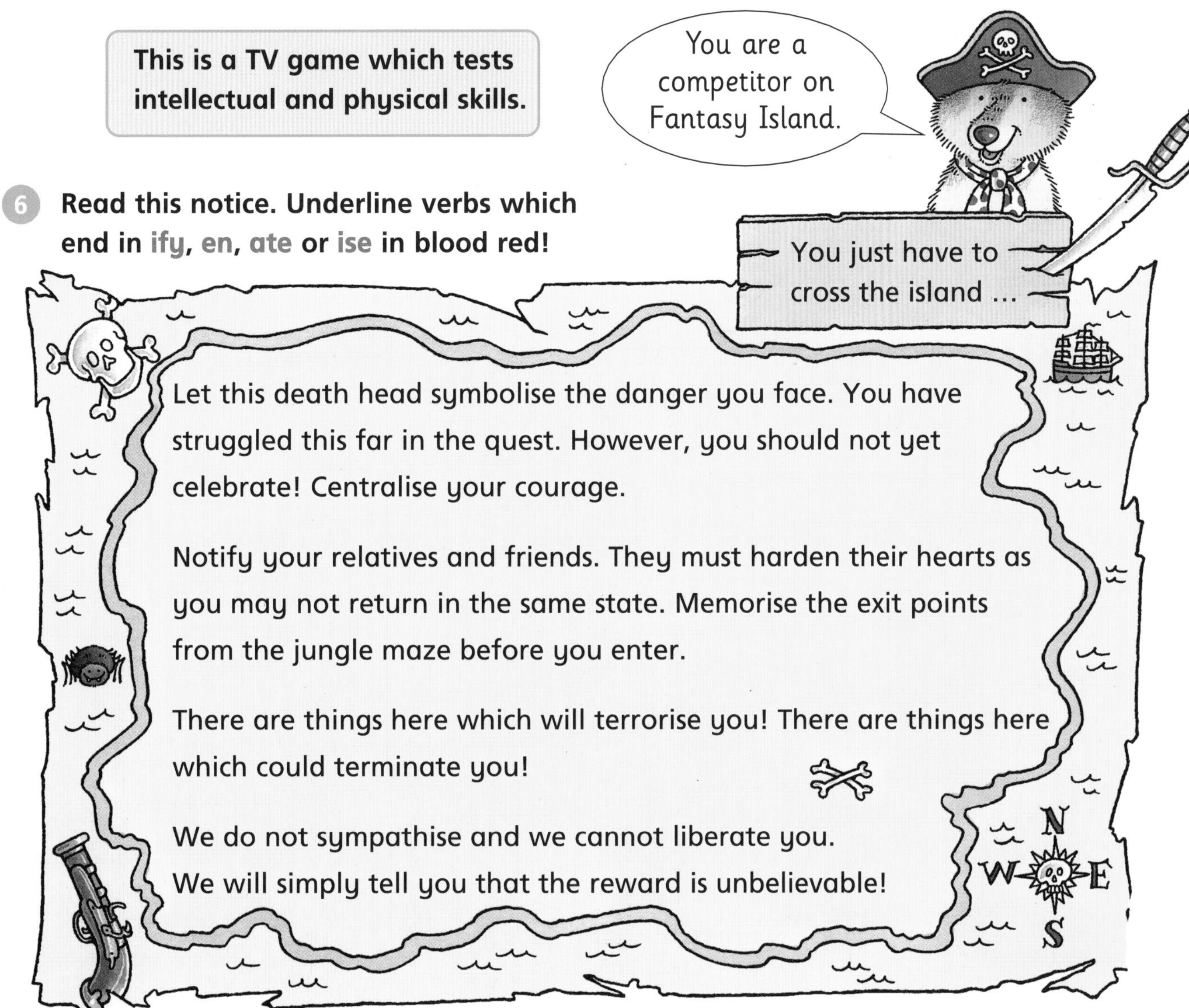

Let this death head symbolise the danger you face. You have struggled this far in the quest. However, you should not yet celebrate! Centralise your courage.

Notify your relatives and friends. They must harden their hearts as you may not return in the same state. Memorise the exit points from the jungle maze before you enter.

There are things here which will terrorise you! There are things here which could terminate you!

We do not sympathise and we cannot liberate you.
We will simply tell you that the reward is unbelievable!

To reinforce this activity, discuss the dangers hinted at in the notice, and try drawing a plan of the island together.

Well done!

Once upon a time

Archaic words are words which are no longer used in everyday language. You can use them in your story writing to give a sense of the past.

Read this glossary of archaic words.

anon – soon
apothecary – chemist
art – are
astride – on a horse
bestrode – rode
betimes – soon
e'er – ever
fair – lovely
forsooth – truly, really
goest – goes
maid – girl
merry – good, happy
motley – jester's clothes
pray, **prithee** – please
steed – horse
thee, **thou** – you
thy, **thine** – yours
unto – to
wherefore – why

Write these speeches in modern English.

Prithee, where goest thou?

Forsooth, thou art a fair maid.

He was as merry a knight as e'er bestrode a steed.

We must go anon!

I must to the apothecary betimes!

Look for archaic language in a Shakespeare play, and encourage your child to experiment with it in her own writing. One way of giving writing a historical feel is to leave out contractions. For example, she could use *cannot* instead of *can't*.

Join them up (2)

There are several sorts of connective. They join pieces of text in different ways.

Connectives of opposition connect opposite sides of an argument

Connectives of time indicate the passage of time

Listing connectives indicate order of importance

Connectives of addition connect more information to the original

Connectives of explanation connect explanatory text to the original

Reinforcing connectives add supporting information

Connectives of result indicate an outcome

Write each of these connectives under the correct heading.

just then for example meanwhile first of all later furthermore firstly that is to say in other words however on the other hand anyway also finally ~~nevertheless~~ ~~besides~~ after all therefore moreover ~~consequently~~ as a result

Explanation	Opposition	Addition	Reinforcing
	nevertheless		besides

Listing	Time	Result
		consequently

Try to find some archaic connectives (e.g. *whomsoever, hereafter*) in the Bible or in legal documents.

Fantastic!

"Now" words

Everyone uses slang.
Some slang words are invented, and some are old words used in a different way.

1 Here are some examples of modern slang.
Tick the box if you agree with the meaning given.
If you don't, write your own meaning.

c'mon – come with me	☐	....
wicked – really interesting	☐	....
yep / yeah – yes	☐	....
smokin'! – really exciting	☐	....
terrific / t'riffic – good	☐	....
cool / well cool – fashionable	☐	....
easy! – that's no problem to me	☐	....
gross – really disgusting	☐	....
dude / guy / bloke – boy / man	☐	....
wo! – I'm surprised	☐	....
chill out – be calm	☐	....
you are so dead – you are in trouble	☐	....

2 Now write four local slang expressions.

....

....

Discuss with your child the slang words you use at home or at work.
Are they the ones you used when you were a child or a teenager?
Make a collection of slang expressions particular to your own region.

New ideas and inventions need new words and phrases.

3 **This alien has not visited Earth for 30 years. Explain what these new words mean.**

compact disc ....

text message ....

Internet ....

mobile phone ....

computer ....

surfing the net ....

fast food ....

laptop ....

Some words go out of usage, and are replaced by others.

4 **Write the correct modern word(s) for each of these.**

washtub ....

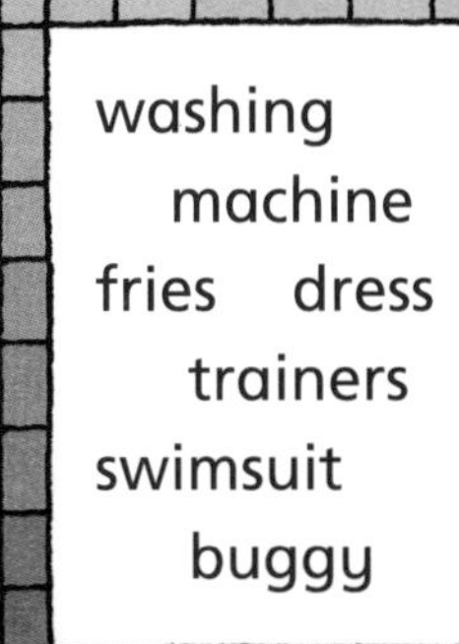

washing machine
fries dress
trainers
swimsuit
buggy

chips ....

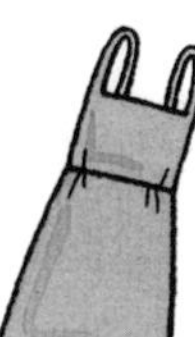

frock ....

pushchair ....

swimming costume ....

pumps ....

Talk to grandparents and other older relatives about the slang they used when they were young. Compare the favourite slang expressions of three generations!

Discuss the slang words children and teenagers use to describe music, clothes, sport or television programmes.

Figures of speech

A **simile** is a way of describing something by comparing it to something else.

1 **Match each adjective to a noun, and write the simile.**

Adjectives
clear ~~bright~~
timid tough
slow

as bright as diamonds ....
....
....
....
....

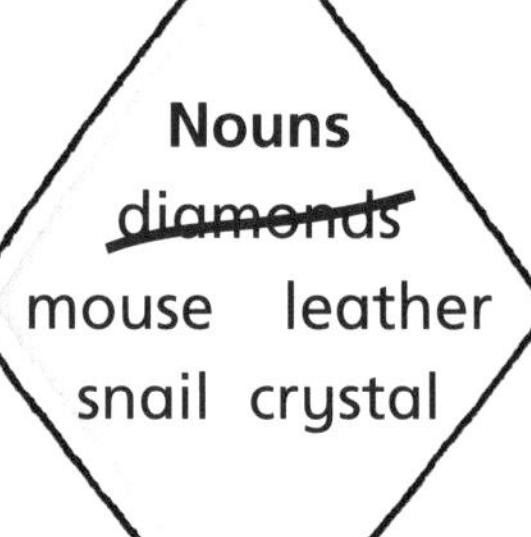

2 **Now complete these similes.**

Some similes use archaic words. You may need to look them up.

as fit as a ....

as happy as a ....

as round as a ....

as black as ....

as straight as a ....

as plain as a ....

ramrod fiddle barrel king coal pikestaff

3 **Use these nouns to make some similes.**

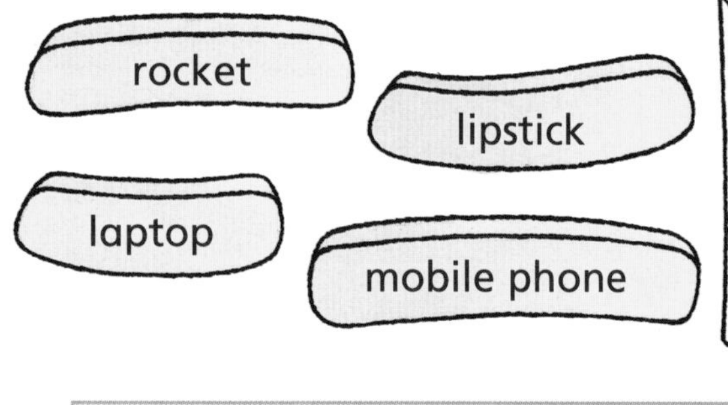

as .... as a ....

as .... as a ....

as .... as a ....

as .... as a ....

Similes are expressed in two ways: *as* ______ *as a* ______ and *like a* __________ . Make up some similes to describe yourselves, other family members, pets or friends. Spot similes in storybooks.

A **metaphor** is a way of describing something by calling it something else.

4 **Read these rhymes, spotting similes and metaphors. Underline the metaphors.**

A note for you …

You are the apple
of my heart,
You are a juicy plum,
I'll let you tidy up
my room,
Because you are my
MUM!

You

Your eyes are as bright as silver stars,
Your hair is the Milky Way,
Your smile is like a rocket launched,
It blasts my heart away!

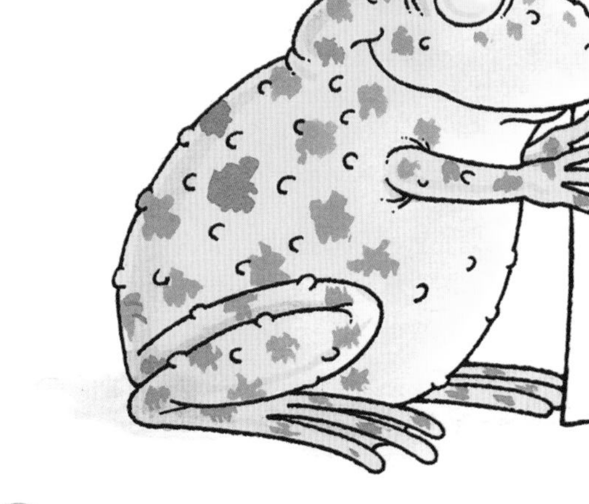

My pet

My pet's eyes are red-hot coals,
His skin is rhino hide,
He's as wobbly as a jellyfish,
That's washed up with the tide.
He's as tough as any rock,
He's as gentle as a dove,
He's a strawberry ice cream sundae,
He fills me up with love!

5 **Write a list of metaphors describing your favourite person.**

Wilma

She is: – a rock
– a swift arrow
– an angel
– a bundle of laughs

Name: ....

is a ....

is a ....

is a ....

is a ....

Metaphors are often used in everyday conversation. For example, a young child might be called *My little lamb*. Metaphors such as *Star buy!* are extensively used in advertising copy. See how many you and your child can spot.

Sparkling!

Proverbs

A **proverb** is a saying which offers advice or guidance in the form of a brief, vivid sentence.

1 What does each of these proverbs mean?

He wants to have his cake and eat it. ....

....

Let sleeping dogs lie. ....

....

2 Match each of these proverbs with its meaning.

Strike while the iron is hot.	E	A penny saved is a pound gained.	
Actions speak louder than words.		More haste, less speed.	
Honesty is the best policy.		Look before you leap.	

Meanings

A Simply saying something doesn't prove you mean it; your actions prove you do!
B Think carefully before you act.
C Dishonesty results in trouble.
D If you don't waste your money on small things it will soon grow as savings.
E Act quickly once your mind is made up.
F If you rush into things without care, you may have to redo them, which slows you down.

Many traditional proverbs are related to farming, the seasons or the weather. *Red sky at night, shepherd's delight; red sky in the morning, shepherd's warning* is an example of this. Contemporary proverbs, such as *What you see is what you get*, may be computer-related.

3 **Read these new proverbs, and write the meaning of each.**

M1 LONDON 25m

There's many a mile down a motorway. There is a long way to go.

A lolly in the hand is worth two in the shop ....

A text in time saves nine. ....

Hello

4 **Now invent some proverbs of your own, based on these subjects.**

fast food	television	pocket money	holidays

5 **Invent two proverbs which include the words shown.**

ice lollies

designer trainers

6 **Write some "family favourite" proverbs here.**

User:

User:

User:

Creative activities like these will extend your child's vocabulary and generate an interest in words.
List the proverbs which each family member likes to quote. Grandparents and other older relatives may know some archaic ones which seem obscure today.

Well done!

Spelling tips

Mnemonics are devices which help you to remember tricky spellings. You can make them up yourself.

I age in marriage.

1 **Match these tricky words with their mnemonics (in the speech bubbles). Write the words in the spaces.**

2 **Invent your own mnemonics for these words. Underline the bits you find tricky first.**

Let your child try out her mnemonics on paper. Playing with words and pictures will produce some interesting ideas. One simple way of remembering a spelling is to write the tricky part of the word in capital letters (e.g. *langUage, wEIght*).

Good thinking!

Word games

A word family is a group of words with the same prefix, root or suffix.

1 **A word search is a good way of remembering words in a word family. Colour the letter squares to show up the words beginning with the prefix sus.**

a	b	s	u	s	p	e	c	t	f
c	d	e	s	u	s	p	e	n	d
i	s	u	s	p	i	c	i	o	n
j	k	l	s	u	s	t	a	i	n

2 **Write these words in the squares in such a way that the letter string eigh is always in the same position on the grid.**

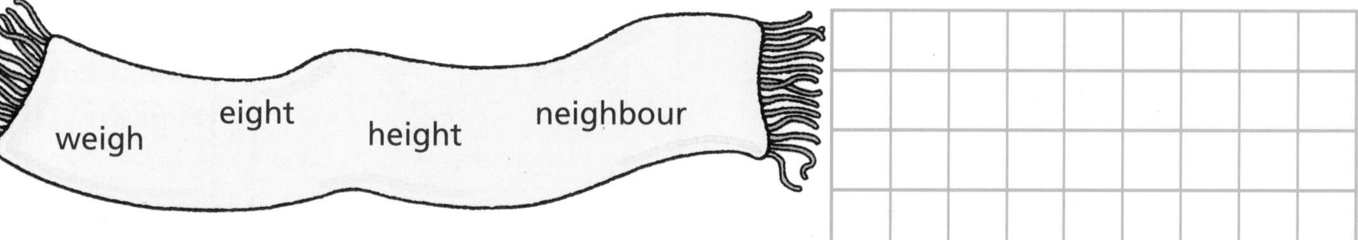

3 **Make word crosses using words with the same spelling pattern. Draw round the finished crosses in a colour.**

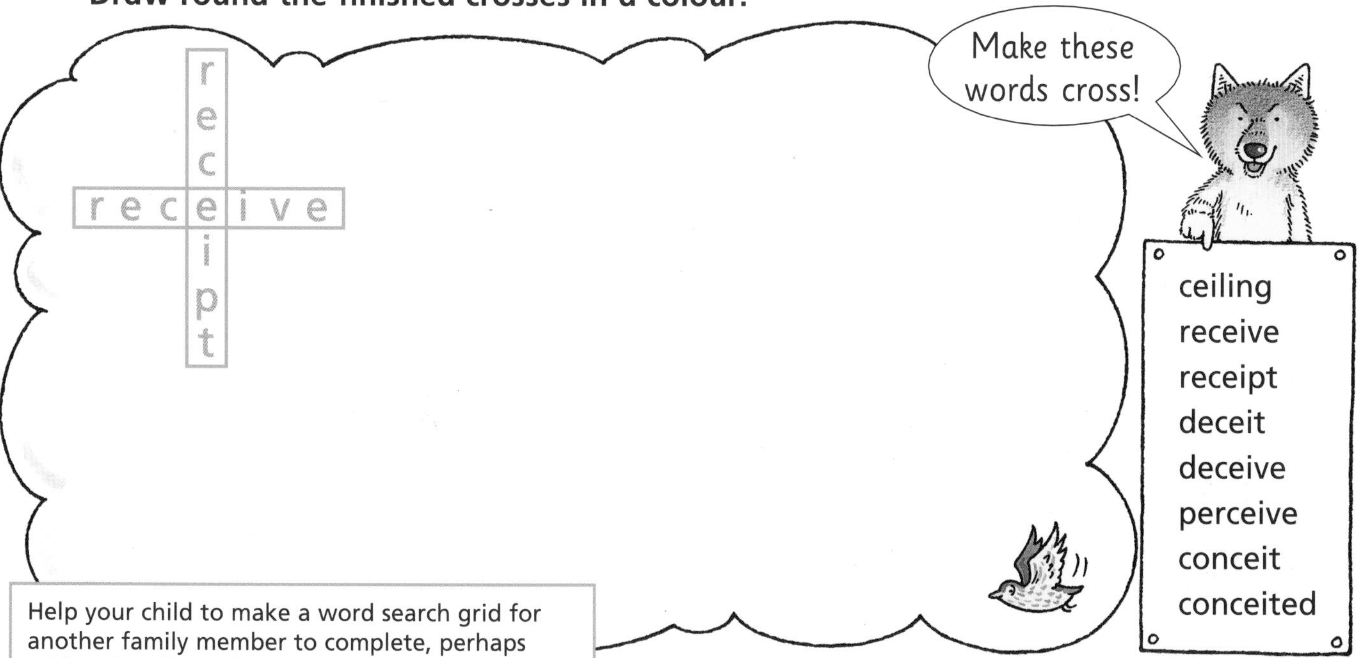

Help your child to make a word search grid for another family member to complete, perhaps with a time limit of one minute.

Word games such as Scrabble will help your child to develop mental agility with letters and words.

Super!

Where is it from?

English uses words from many other languages.

English Language Melting Pot

Gaelic French Greek Turkish Ancient Greek Italian Spanish American English Australian English Hindi

1 All these words are about food. Write each word under the correct heading. Use a dictionary if you need to.

restaurant buffet taramasalata pizza paella barbie croissant yoghurt spaghetti moussaka shish kebab pasta hummus tortilla fast food gazpacho baguette

American English	Spanish	Turkish	Greek	Australian English

Italian	French

Some old British surnames came from the name of a place, or a family member, or an occupation.

I'm John from the hill.

I'm John from the wood.

Forest
Wood
Lea
Ford
Hill
⋮

I'm Walter Wolfson!

2 Can you think of any more surnames based on places?

....

....

3 Make up some new surnames based on places.

....

....

Look through the telephone directory together, working out where some of the surnames come from.
Look up the names of unusual foods in the dictionary, noting the origins of the words.

I'm John Hunter.

4 **Complete this crossword.**
All the solutions are surnames derived from medieval occupations.

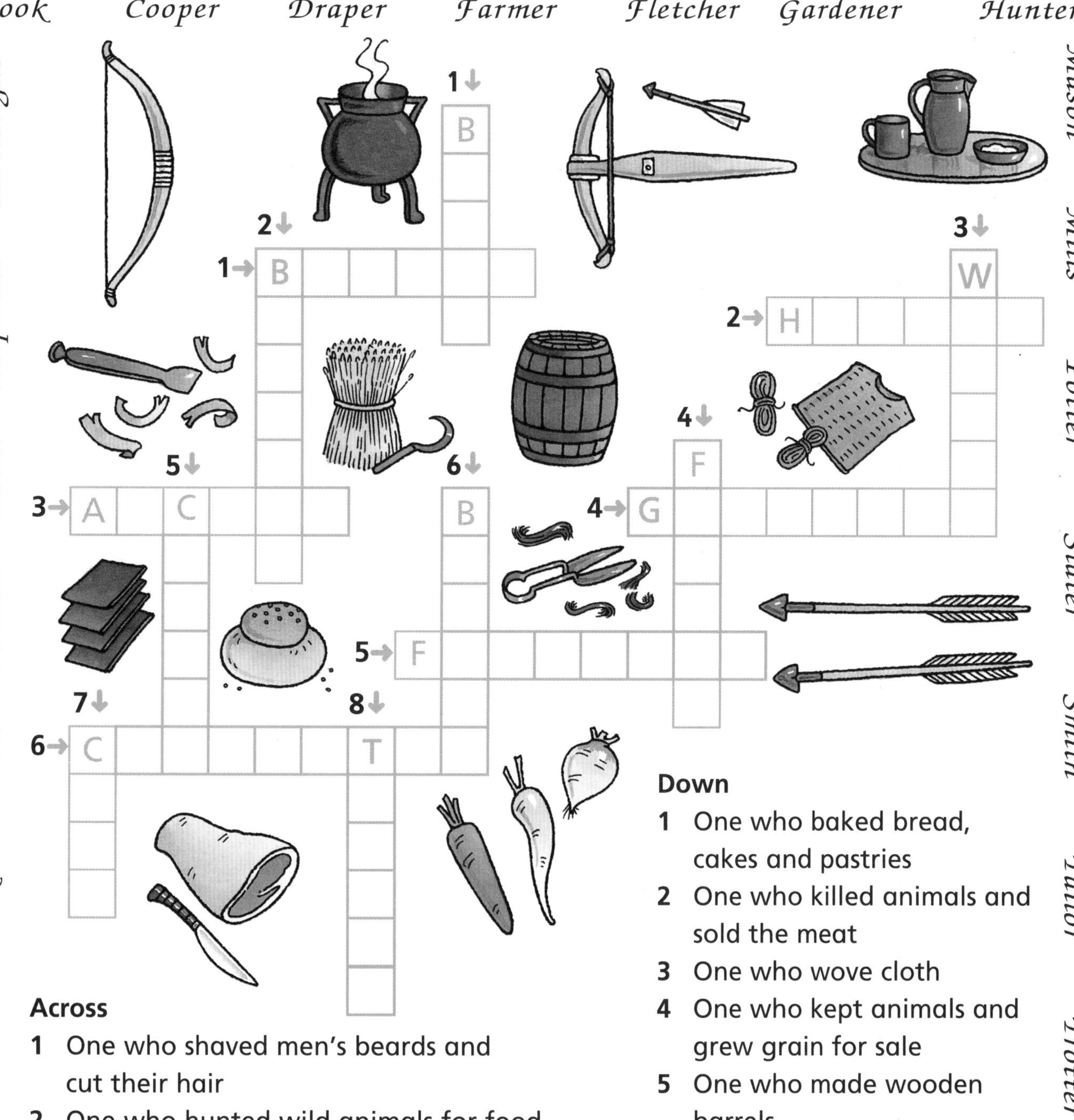

Across

1 One who shaved men's beards and cut their hair
2 One who hunted wild animals for food
3 A soldier who used a bow and arrow
4 One who grew plants for food or decoration
5 One who made arrows
6 One who made objects from wood

Down

1 One who baked bread, cakes and pastries
2 One who killed animals and sold the meat
3 One who wove cloth
4 One who kept animals and grew grain for sale
5 One who made wooden barrels
6 A servant in charge of the wine cellar
7 One who cooked the meals
8 One who made clothes

All the medieval British surnames in this crossword are derived from traditional occupations. Many of them have Norman (French) or Roman (Latin) origins. Discuss possible career choices for your child, making up surnames relating to contemporary jobs (e.g. *Pilot*, *Programmer*).

Wolves were a symbol of strength for the Romans.

Words from Ancient Greek and Latin are used as English roots, prefixes and suffixes.

5 Read these Latin and Greek roots and their meanings.
Look at the words on the shields, and write each word on the correct line.

Latin	Meaning	English	
scribo	write	scribble	....
specto	look	....	....
video	see	....	....
libertas	freedom	....	....
civis	citizen	....	....
excito	awake	....	....
medicus	doctor	....	....
dicto	compose	....	....
custodio	guard	....	....
architectus	builder	....	....
antiquus	ancient	....	....
Greek			
phone	sound	....	....
photo	light	....	....
scope	see	....	....
auto	self	....	....
aster	star	....	....

spectate scribble spectacle script

video liberty liberate videotape

civil civic excite excited

medicine dictate medical diction

architecture custody architect custodian

antique antiquity phoned telephone

photograph telephoto microscope periscope

autopilot automatic asteroid astronaut

If possible, look at an English-Latin or an English-Ancient Greek dictionary together. See how many of the Latin or Greek words have influenced English words.

Spectacular!

Word puzzles

1 **Cut up these long words to make shorter ones.**
Make as many as you can.

educationally

2 **Look at these long words.**
Cross out the short words which can't be made from their letters.

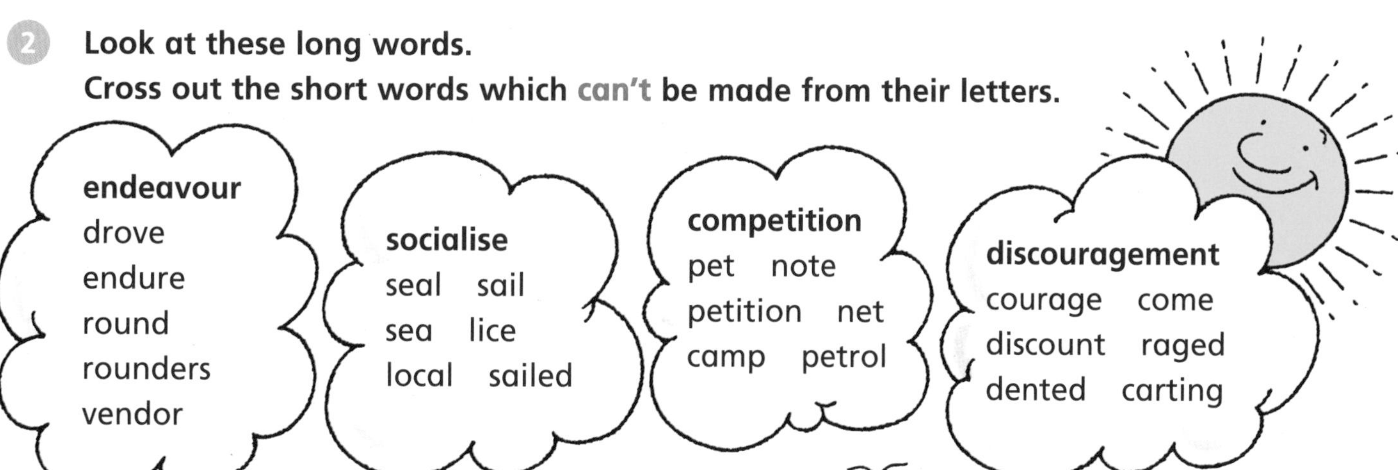

3 **Try this three-word challenge. Write three words with each of the prefixes.**

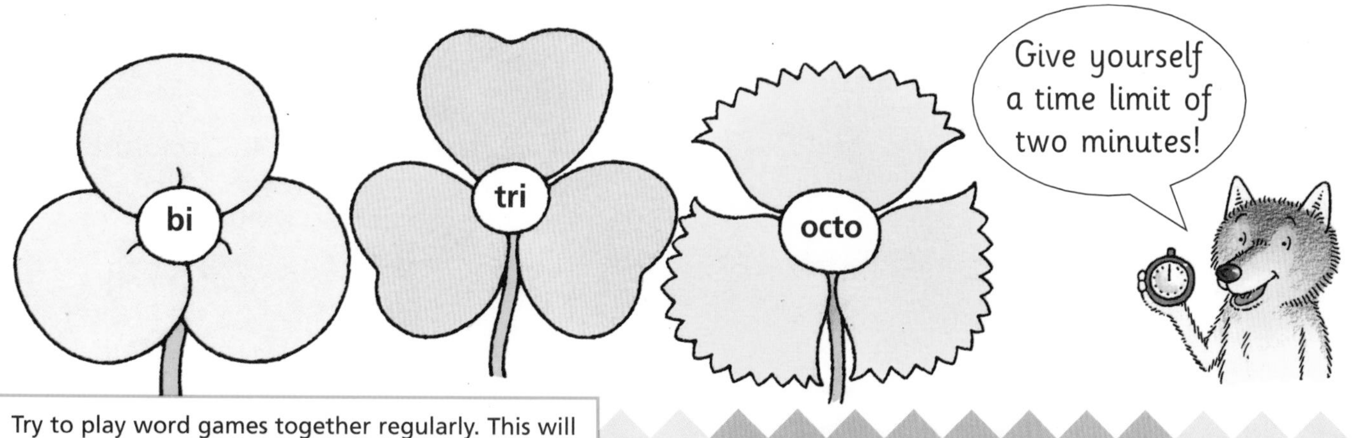

Try to play word games together regularly. This will develop your child's memory and mental agility, extend her vocabulary and help her with spelling.

Well done!

What's the vowel?

An **unstressed vowel** is one which cannot be heard clearly because that part of the word is spoken so quickly.

tel<u>e</u>vision

1 **Complete each of these words with its unstressed vowel(s).**

START

skel......ton d......scribe hol......day tel......vision

env......lope trav......l hist......ry

diction......ry parl......ament bus......ness

sep......rate jewell......ry Sat......rday veg......t......ble N......vember Aug......st slal......m look......d D......cember wellingt......n

FINISH

business	history
dictionary	travel

skeleton	television
describe	envelope
holiday	August

November	separate
parliament	Saturday
jewellery	

vegetable
looked
December
wellington
slalom

2 **Each of the words on the left contains an unstressed vowel. In the word on the right, the same vowel is stressed. Write the vowel to complete the word.**

telephone	tel......phonist
competition	comp......titive
signify	sign......ficant
secretary	secret......rial

A knowledge of stressed and unstressed vowels can help your child with spelling, as he will be able to group words according to their spelling rather than their pronunciation.
Regional accent can influence the way in which people stress vowels. Check the Standard English pronunciation in a dictionary.

Excellent!

Skills test

Write the answers to these.

1. Drums, cymbals and triangles are all this kind of instrument. ....
2. The air is made dirty by this. ....
3. Easy to bend ....
4. An interesting find ....
5. A list of words and meanings in alphabetical order ....
6. The root of **beautifully** ....
7. A flying vehicle with wings ....
8. The verb form of **personal** ....
9. The verb form of **celebrity** ....
10. The verb form of **beauty** ....
11. Write the connective. **We went walking; however, it was difficult.** ....
12. Write the connective. **It was dark, although early evening.** ....
13. What do the archaic words **thee** and **thou** mean? ....
14. The root of **telescope** ....

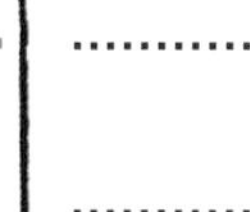

What do these prefixes mean?

15. **bi** ....
16. **il** ....
17. **trans** ....
18. **audi** ....

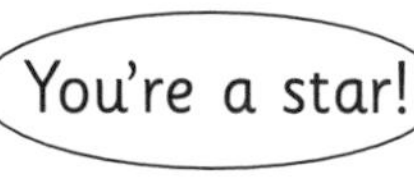

Encourage your child to concentrate on this test, but don't let him become anxious about it. Praise all his efforts!

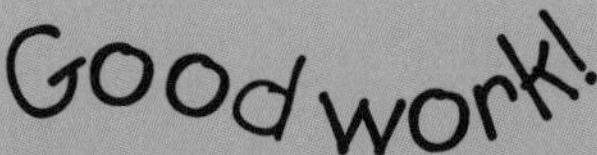

Answers

Pages 2-3
1 nation
station
formation
translation
education

completion
depletion
deletion
excretion
secretion

repetition
position
competition
opposition
petition

motion
devotion
notion
lotion
emotion

contribution
distribution
revolution
pollution
institution

2 passion mission
lotion motion
oppression profession
proportion reduction
magician optician
percussion session
infusion explosion
exclusion confusion

Pages 4-5
1 triangle
angled
rectangle
quadrangle

justice
injustice
justification
adjust

uncover
covering
recover
discover

personal
personally
personality
personify

excellently
excelled
excellency
excelling

unclear
clearly
clearing
cleared

unfit
fitted
fittest
refit

2 *Make sure the root words have been used.*
3 forgive obey
thank honest
build gallop
joy open
delight child
approve like

Pages 6-7
1 aerial crucial pictorial
marsupial Centennial
genial jovial arterial
biennial Industrial
terrestrial editorial
2 miserable probable
teachable available reliable
enjoyable laughable
avoidable agreeable
washable
3 Visible!
Possible but not sensible!
He's irresistible!
He's indestructible!
I'm flexible and collapsible!

Pages 8-9
1 aqualung aeroplane
transport supersonic
rewind megastore
prehistoric pronoun
2-3 *Make sure that the prefixes (green) are paired with root words (red).*

Pages 10-11
1-3 *Make sure the words are correctly spelled.*
4 sta/tion/er/y cook/er/y
flow/er/y pow/der/y
pa/per/y lott/er/y
up/holst/er/y sadd/ler/y
butt/er/y
Make sure the words are correctly spelled.
5 *Make sure the words are correctly spelled.*
6 *Red*: green rook mock
cook trick rock crock witch
Blue: ery *in each case*

Pages 12-13
1 *Blue*: furthermore
anyway meanwhile
however
Red: on the other hand
in addition to
for example in other words
Green: also if because
finally so and yet
2 more / over mean / while
what / ever further / more
who / ever when / ever
there / fore any / way
how / ever be / sides
where / as never / the / less
Make sure the words are correctly spelled.
3 because nevertheless
when whatever
furthermore in fact
whereas however but

Pages 14-15
1 blacken soften
toughen harden
deafen deaden
2 silken golden lumpen
3 glamourise terrorise
capitalise symbolise
pressurise memorise
sympathise summarise
4 vaccinate liberate
narrate orchestrate
celebrate gravitate
decorate medicate
5 *Red*: notify mummify
beautify identity
Blue: notice mummy
beauty identity
6 *Red*: symbolise celebrate
centralise notify harden
memorise terrorise
terminate sympathise
liberate

Page 16
Where are you going, please?
You really are a lovely girl.
He was as good / happy a knight as ever rode a horse.
We must go soon!
I must go to the chemist soon.

Page 17
Connectives of explanation:
for example that is to say
in other words
Connectives of opposition:
however
on the other hand
Connectives of addition:
furthermore also moreover
Reinforcing connectives:
anyway after all
Listing connectives:
first of all firstly finally
Connectives of time:
just then meanwhile later
Connectives of result:
therefore as a result

Pages 18-19
1-2 *free choice*
3 a small disc from which recorded sound is produced by a laser beam
a printed message on the screen of a mobile phone
an electronic system for sending information from computer to computer
a cordless phone which can be used anywhere
an electronic machine used to store and analyse information
going through different pieces of information available on the Internet
snack food served very quickly from cafés
a small, portable computer
4 washtub - washing machine
chips - fries
frock - dress
swimming costume - swimsuit
pushchair - buggy
pumps - trainers

Pages 20-21
1 as bright as diamonds
as clear as crystal
as timid as a mouse
as tough as leather
as slow as a snail
2 as fit as a fiddle
as happy as a king
as round as a barrel
as black as coal
as straight as a ramrod
as plain as a pikestaff
3 *free choice*
4 You are the apple of my heart
You are a juicy plum
Your hair is the Milky Way
It blasts my heart away
My pet's eyes are red-hot coals
His skin is rhino hide
He's a strawberry ice cream sundae
He fills me up with love
5 *free choice*

Pages 22-23
1 He wants to have it both ways.
If something is settled, leave it alone.
2 E D
A F
C B
3 It's better to have just one thing than to be hoping for two.
A small action, taken early enough, can prevent trouble later.
4-6 *free choice*

Page 24
1 Not a narrow book but a story - narrative
Someone I like to the end! - friend
Looks like sky - science
Don't be late for this! - chocolate
I want words with you - sword
2 *free choice*

Page 25
1 suspect
suspend
suspicion
sustain
2 weigh
eight
height
neighbour
3 *Make sure the words are correctly spelled.*

Pages 26-28
1 *American English*:
fast food
Spanish: paella
tortilla gazpacho
Turkish: yoghurt
shish kebab hummus
Greek: taramasalata
moussaka
Italian: pizza
spaghetti pasta
French: restaurant buffet
croissant baguette
Australian English: barbie
2-3 *free choice*
4 *Across*
1 BARBER 2 HUNTER
3 ARCHER 4 GARDENER
5 FLETCHER 6 CARPENTER
Down
1 BAKER 2 BUTCHER
3 WEAVER 4 FARMER
5 COOPER 6 BUTLER
7 COOK 8 TAILOR
5 *Check that the words have been written on the correct lines.*

Page 29
1 *Check that each letter has been used once only in each word.*
2 rounders local sailed
camp petrol dented
3 *Make sure the prefixes have been used correctly.*

Page 30
1 skeleton describe holiday
television envelope travel
history business parliament
dictionary separate
jewellery Saturday
vegetable November
August slalom looked
December wellington
2 telephonist competitive
significant secretarial

Page 31
1 percussion
2 pollution
3 flexible
4 discovery
5 dictionary
6 beauty
7 aeroplane
8 personify / personalise
9 celebrate
10 beautify
11 however
12 although
13 you
14 scope
15 twice
16 not
17 across
18 relating to sound